Supe

Driving Logbook

This Driving Log Belongs to:

_____

Learn to Drive Pre-Start Checklist

- ☐ Secure Mobile Device
- ☐ Key in Ignition
- ☐ Adjust Seat
- ☐ Doors Closed and Locked
- ☐ Adjust Head Rest
- ☐ Adjust Mirrors
- ☐ Adjust Vents
- ☐ Adjust Temperature Controls
- ☐ Adjust Steering Wheel
- ☐ Fasten Seat Belts

"Drive Defensively"
www.driveredcoach.com

DEFENSIVE DRIVING PRINCIPLES

FOLLWING DISTANCE (2-4 SEC.)

VISUAL LEAD TIME (12-20 SEC.)

SEE AND BE SEEN

HAVE AN ESCAPE ROUTE

PREDICT THE WORST

ISOLATE YOUR VEHICLE

ALWAYS WEAR YOUR SEATBELT

DRIVING SKILLS TO PRACTICE

- [ ] TURNING
- [ ] INTERSECTIONS
- [ ] PARALLEL PARKING
- [ ] 3 POINT TURN
- [ ] CITY DRIVING
- [ ] EXPESSWAYS
- [ ] RURAL DRIVING
- [ ] BACKING
- [ ] NIGHT DRIVING
- [ ] EMERGENCY PROCEDURES

Learn How to Drive
www.driveredcoach.com

Daily Driving Report

DATE: _____

LOCATION OF DRIVE: _____

SKILLS PRACTICED:

NOTES ON THE DRIVE:

TOTAL DRIVING TIME

Today's drive total		Accumulated Time	

SIGNATURE OF ADULT:

_____

Daily Driving Report

DATE: _____

LOCATION OF DRIVE: _____

SKILLS PRACTICED:	NOTES ON THE DRIVE:

TOTAL DRIVING TIME

Today's drive total		Accumulated Time	

SIGNATURE OF ADULT:

_____

Daily Driving Report

DATE: _____

LOCATION OF DRIVE: _____

SKILLS PRACTICED:	NOTES ON THE DRIVE:

TOTAL DRIVING TIME

Today's drive total		Accumulated Time	

SIGNATURE OF ADULT:

_____

Daily Driving Report

DATE: _____

LOCATION OF DRIVE: _____

SKILLS PRACTICED:	NOTES ON THE DRIVE:

TOTAL DRIVING TIME

Today's drive total		Accumulated Time	

SIGNATURE OF ADULT:

_____

Daily Driving Report

DATE: _____

LOCATION OF DRIVE: _____

SKILLS PRACTICED:	NOTES ON THE DRIVE:

TOTAL DRIVING TIME

Today's drive total		Accumulated Time	

SIGNATURE OF ADULT:

_____

Daily Driving Report

DATE: _____

LOCATION OF DRIVE: _____

SKILLS PRACTICED:	NOTES ON THE DRIVE:

TOTAL DRIVING TIME

Today's drive total		Accumulated Time	

SIGNATURE OF ADULT:

_____

Daily Driving Report

DATE: _____

LOCATION OF DRIVE: _____

SKILLS PRACTICED:	NOTES ON THE DRIVE:

TOTAL DRIVING TIME

Today's drive total		Accumulated Time	

SIGNATURE OF ADULT:

_____

Daily Driving Report

DATE: _____

LOCATION OF DRIVE: _____

SKILLS PRACTICED:	NOTES ON THE DRIVE:

TOTAL DRIVING TIME

Today's drive total		Accumulated Time	

SIGNATURE OF ADULT:

_____

Daily Driving Report

DATE: _____

LOCATION OF DRIVE: _____

SKILLS PRACTICED:	NOTES ON THE DRIVE:

TOTAL DRIVING TIME

Today's drive total		Accumulated Time	

SIGNATURE OF ADULT:

_____

Daily Driving Report

DATE: _____

LOCATION OF DRIVE: _____

SKILLS PRACTICED:	NOTES ON THE DRIVE:

TOTAL DRIVING TIME

Today's drive total		Accumulated Time	

SIGNATURE OF ADULT:

_____

Daily Driving Report

DATE: _____

LOCATION OF DRIVE: _____

SKILLS PRACTICED:	NOTES ON THE DRIVE:

TOTAL DRIVING TIME

Today's drive total		Accumulated Time	

SIGNATURE OF ADULT:

_____

Daily Driving Report

DATE: _____

LOCATION OF DRIVE: _____

SKILLS PRACTICED:	NOTES ON THE DRIVE:

TOTAL DRIVING TIME

Today's drive total		Accumulated Time	

SIGNATURE OF ADULT:

_____

Daily Driving Report

DATE: _____

LOCATION OF DRIVE: _____

SKILLS PRACTICED:	NOTES ON THE DRIVE:

TOTAL DRIVING TIME

Today's drive total		Accumulated Time	

SIGNATURE OF ADULT:

_____

Daily Driving Report

DATE: _____

LOCATION OF DRIVE: _____

SKILLS PRACTICED:	NOTES ON THE DRIVE:

TOTAL DRIVING TIME

Today's drive total		Accumulated Time	

SIGNATURE OF ADULT:

_____

Daily Driving Report

DATE: _____

LOCATION OF DRIVE: _____

SKILLS PRACTICED:	NOTES ON THE DRIVE:

TOTAL DRIVING TIME

Today's drive total		Accumulated Time	

SIGNATURE OF ADULT:

_____

Daily Driving Report

DATE: _____

LOCATION OF DRIVE: _____

SKILLS PRACTICED:	NOTES ON THE DRIVE:

TOTAL DRIVING TIME

Today's drive total		Accumulated Time	

SIGNATURE OF ADULT:

_____

Daily Driving Report

DATE: _____

LOCATION OF DRIVE: _____

SKILLS PRACTICED:	NOTES ON THE DRIVE:

TOTAL DRIVING TIME

Today's drive total		Accumulated Time	

SIGNATURE OF ADULT:

_____

Daily Driving Report

DATE: _____

LOCATION OF DRIVE: _____

SKILLS PRACTICED:	NOTES ON THE DRIVE:

TOTAL DRIVING TIME

Today's drive total		Accumulated Time	

SIGNATURE OF ADULT:

_____

Daily Driving Report

DATE: _____

LOCATION OF DRIVE: _____

SKILLS PRACTICED:	NOTES ON THE DRIVE:

TOTAL DRIVING TIME

Today's drive total		Accumulated Time	

SIGNATURE OF ADULT:

_____

Daily Driving Report

DATE: _____

LOCATION OF DRIVE: _____

SKILLS PRACTICED:	NOTES ON THE DRIVE:

TOTAL DRIVING TIME

Today's drive total		Accumulated Time	

SIGNATURE OF ADULT:

_____

Daily Driving Report

DATE: _____

LOCATION OF DRIVE: _____

SKILLS PRACTICED:	NOTES ON THE DRIVE:

TOTAL DRIVING TIME

Today's drive total		Accumulated Time	

SIGNATURE OF ADULT:

_____

Daily Driving Report

DATE:

LOCATION OF DRIVE:

SKILLS PRACTICED:

NOTES ON THE DRIVE:

TOTAL DRIVING TIME

Today's drive total

Accumulated Time

SIGNATURE OF ADULT:

Daily Driving Report

DATE: _____

LOCATION OF DRIVE: _____

SKILLS PRACTICED:	NOTES ON THE DRIVE:

TOTAL DRIVING TIME

Today's drive total		Accumulated Time	

SIGNATURE OF ADULT:

_____

Daily Driving Report

DATE:

LOCATION OF DRIVE:

SKILLS PRACTICED:

NOTES ON THE DRIVE:

TOTAL DRIVING TIME

Today's drive total

Accumulated Time

SIGNATURE OF ADULT:

Daily Driving Report

DATE: _____

LOCATION OF DRIVE: _____

SKILLS PRACTICED:	NOTES ON THE DRIVE:

TOTAL DRIVING TIME

Today's drive total		Accumulated Time	

SIGNATURE OF ADULT:

_____

Daily Driving Report

DATE:

LOCATION OF DRIVE:

SKILLS PRACTICED:

NOTES ON THE DRIVE:

TOTAL DRIVING TIME

Today's drive total

Accumulated Time

SIGNATURE OF ADULT:

Daily Driving Report

DATE: _____

LOCATION OF DRIVE: _____

SKILLS PRACTICED:	NOTES ON THE DRIVE:

TOTAL DRIVING TIME

Today's drive total		Accumulated Time	

SIGNATURE OF ADULT:

_____

Daily Driving Report

DATE: _____

LOCATION OF DRIVE: _____

SKILLS PRACTICED:	NOTES ON THE DRIVE:

TOTAL DRIVING TIME

Today's drive total		Accumulated Time	

SIGNATURE OF ADULT:

_____

Daily Driving Report

DATE: _____

LOCATION OF DRIVE: _____

SKILLS PRACTICED:	NOTES ON THE DRIVE:

TOTAL DRIVING TIME

Today's drive total		Accumulated Time	

SIGNATURE OF ADULT:

_____

Daily Driving Report

DATE: _____

LOCATION OF DRIVE: _____

SKILLS PRACTICED:	NOTES ON THE DRIVE:

TOTAL DRIVING TIME

Today's drive total		Accumulated Time	

SIGNATURE OF ADULT:

_____

Daily Driving Report

DATE: _____

LOCATION OF DRIVE: _____

SKILLS PRACTICED:	NOTES ON THE DRIVE:

TOTAL DRIVING TIME

Today's drive total		Accumulated Time	

SIGNATURE OF ADULT:

_____

Daily Driving Report

DATE: _____

LOCATION OF DRIVE: _____

SKILLS PRACTICED:	NOTES ON THE DRIVE:

TOTAL DRIVING TIME

Today's drive total		Accumulated Time	

SIGNATURE OF ADULT:

_____

Daily Driving Report

DATE:

LOCATION OF DRIVE:

SKILLS PRACTICED:

NOTES ON THE DRIVE:

TOTAL DRIVING TIME

Today's drive total

Accumulated Time

SIGNATURE OF ADULT:

Daily Driving Report

DATE: _____

LOCATION OF DRIVE: _____

SKILLS PRACTICED:	NOTES ON THE DRIVE:

TOTAL DRIVING TIME

Today's drive total		Accumulated Time	

SIGNATURE OF ADULT:

_____

Daily Driving Report

DATE: _____

LOCATION OF DRIVE: _____

SKILLS PRACTICED:	NOTES ON THE DRIVE:

TOTAL DRIVING TIME

Today's drive total		Accumulated Time	

SIGNATURE OF ADULT:

_____

Daily Driving Report

DATE: _____

LOCATION OF DRIVE: _____

SKILLS PRACTICED:	NOTES ON THE DRIVE:

TOTAL DRIVING TIME

Today's drive total		Accumulated Time	

SIGNATURE OF ADULT:

_____

Daily Driving Report

DATE:

LOCATION OF DRIVE:

SKILLS PRACTICED:

NOTES ON THE DRIVE:

TOTAL DRIVING TIME

Today's drive total

Accumulated Time

SIGNATURE OF ADULT:

Daily Driving Report

DATE: _____

LOCATION OF DRIVE: _____

SKILLS PRACTICED:	NOTES ON THE DRIVE:

TOTAL DRIVING TIME

Today's drive total		Accumulated Time	

SIGNATURE OF ADULT:

_____

Daily Driving Report

DATE: ....

LOCATION OF DRIVE: ....

SKILLS
PRACTICED:

NOTES ON THE
DRIVE:

TOTAL DRIVING TIME

Today's
drive
total

Accumulated
Time

SIGNATURE OF ADULT:

....

Daily Driving Report

DATE: _____

LOCATION OF DRIVE: _____

SKILLS PRACTICED:	NOTES ON THE DRIVE:

TOTAL DRIVING TIME

Today's drive total		Accumulated Time	

SIGNATURE OF ADULT:

_____

Daily Driving Report

DATE: _____

LOCATION OF DRIVE: _____

SKILLS PRACTICED:	NOTES ON THE DRIVE:

TOTAL DRIVING TIME

Today's drive total		Accumulated Time	

SIGNATURE OF ADULT:

_____

Daily Driving Report

DATE: _____

LOCATION OF DRIVE: _____

SKILLS PRACTICED:	NOTES ON THE DRIVE:

TOTAL DRIVING TIME

Today's drive total		Accumulated Time	

SIGNATURE OF ADULT:

_____

Daily Driving Report

DATE: ....

LOCATION OF DRIVE: ....

SKILLS PRACTICED:	NOTES ON THE DRIVE:

TOTAL DRIVING TIME

Today's drive total		Accumulated Time	

SIGNATURE OF ADULT:

....

Daily Driving Report

DATE: _____

LOCATION OF DRIVE: _____

SKILLS PRACTICED:	NOTES ON THE DRIVE:

TOTAL DRIVING TIME

Today's drive total		Accumulated Time	

SIGNATURE OF ADULT:

_____

Daily Driving Report

DATE: _____

LOCATION OF DRIVE: _____

SKILLS PRACTICED:

NOTES ON THE DRIVE:

TOTAL DRIVING TIME

Today's drive total		Accumulated Time	

SIGNATURE OF ADULT:

_____

Daily Driving Report

DATE: _____

LOCATION OF DRIVE: _____

SKILLS PRACTICED:

NOTES ON THE DRIVE:

TOTAL DRIVING TIME

Today's drive total		Accumulated Time	

SIGNATURE OF ADULT:

_____

Daily Driving Report

DATE:

LOCATION OF DRIVE:

SKILLS PRACTICED:	NOTES ON THE DRIVE:

TOTAL DRIVING TIME

Today's drive total		Accumulated Time	

SIGNATURE OF ADULT:

Daily Driving Report

DATE: _____

LOCATION OF DRIVE: _____

SKILLS PRACTICED:	NOTES ON THE DRIVE:

TOTAL DRIVING TIME

Today's drive total		Accumulated Time	

SIGNATURE OF ADULT:

_____

Daily Driving Report

DATE: _____

LOCATION OF DRIVE: _____

SKILLS PRACTICED:	NOTES ON THE DRIVE:

TOTAL DRIVING TIME

Today's drive total		Accumulated Time	

SIGNATURE OF ADULT:

_____

Daily Driving Report

DATE: _____

LOCATION OF DRIVE: _____

SKILLS PRACTICED:	NOTES ON THE DRIVE:

TOTAL DRIVING TIME

Today's drive total		Accumulated Time	

SIGNATURE OF ADULT:

_____

Daily Driving Report

DATE: _____

LOCATION OF DRIVE: _____

SKILLS PRACTICED:	NOTES ON THE DRIVE:

TOTAL DRIVING TIME

Today's drive total		Accumulated Time	

SIGNATURE OF ADULT:

_____

Daily Driving Report

DATE: _____

LOCATION OF DRIVE: _____

SKILLS PRACTICED:	NOTES ON THE DRIVE:

TOTAL DRIVING TIME

Today's drive total		Accumulated Time	

SIGNATURE OF ADULT:

_____

Daily Driving Report

DATE: _____

LOCATION OF DRIVE: _____

SKILLS PRACTICED:	NOTES ON THE DRIVE:

TOTAL DRIVING TIME

Today's drive total		Accumulated Time	

SIGNATURE OF ADULT:

_____

Daily Driving Report

DATE: _____

LOCATION OF DRIVE: _____

SKILLS PRACTICED:	NOTES ON THE DRIVE:

TOTAL DRIVING TIME

Today's drive total		Accumulated Time	

SIGNATURE OF ADULT:

_____

Daily Driving Report

DATE: _____

LOCATION OF DRIVE: _____

SKILLS PRACTICED:	NOTES ON THE DRIVE:

TOTAL DRIVING TIME

Today's drive total		Accumulated Time	

SIGNATURE OF ADULT:

_____

Daily Driving Report

DATE: _____

LOCATION OF DRIVE: _____

SKILLS PRACTICED:	NOTES ON THE DRIVE:

TOTAL DRIVING TIME

Today's drive total		Accumulated Time	

SIGNATURE OF ADULT:

_____

Daily Driving Report

DATE: _____

LOCATION OF DRIVE: _____

SKILLS PRACTICED:

NOTES ON THE DRIVE:

TOTAL DRIVING TIME

Today's drive total		Accumulated Time	

SIGNATURE OF ADULT:

_____

Daily Driving Report

DATE:

LOCATION OF DRIVE:

SKILLS PRACTICED:	NOTES ON THE DRIVE:

TOTAL DRIVING TIME

Today's drive total   Accumulated Time

SIGNATURE OF ADULT:

Daily Driving Report

DATE: _____

LOCATION OF DRIVE: _____

SKILLS PRACTICED:	NOTES ON THE DRIVE:

TOTAL DRIVING TIME

Today's drive total		Accumulated Time	

SIGNATURE OF ADULT:

_____

Daily Driving Report

DATE:

LOCATION OF DRIVE:

SKILLS PRACTICED:

NOTES ON THE DRIVE:

TOTAL DRIVING TIME

Today's drive total		Accumulated Time	

SIGNATURE OF ADULT:

Daily Driving Report

DATE: _____

LOCATION OF DRIVE: _____

SKILLS PRACTICED:

NOTES ON THE DRIVE:

TOTAL DRIVING TIME

Today's drive total

Accumulated Time

SIGNATURE OF ADULT:

_____

Daily Driving Report

DATE:

LOCATION OF DRIVE:

SKILLS PRACTICED:	NOTES ON THE DRIVE:

TOTAL DRIVING TIME

Today's drive total		Accumulated Time	

SIGNATURE OF ADULT:

Daily Driving Report

DATE: _____

LOCATION OF DRIVE: _____

SKILLS PRACTICED:

NOTES ON THE DRIVE:

TOTAL DRIVING TIME

Today's drive total		Accumulated Time	

SIGNATURE OF ADULT:

_____

Daily Driving Report

DATE:

LOCATION OF DRIVE:

SKILLS PRACTICED:	NOTES ON THE DRIVE:

TOTAL DRIVING TIME

Today's drive total		Accumulated Time	

SIGNATURE OF ADULT:

Daily Driving Report

DATE: _____

LOCATION OF DRIVE: _____

SKILLS PRACTICED:	NOTES ON THE DRIVE:

TOTAL DRIVING TIME

Today's drive total		Accumulated Time	

SIGNATURE OF ADULT:

_____

Daily Driving Report

DATE: _____

LOCATION OF DRIVE: _____

SKILLS PRACTICED:	NOTES ON THE DRIVE:

TOTAL DRIVING TIME

Today's drive total		Accumulated Time	

SIGNATURE OF ADULT:

_____

Daily Driving Report

DATE: _____

LOCATION OF DRIVE: _____

SKILLS PRACTICED:	NOTES ON THE DRIVE:

TOTAL DRIVING TIME

Today's drive total		Accumulated Time	

SIGNATURE OF ADULT:

_____

Daily Driving Report

DATE: _____

LOCATION OF DRIVE: _____

SKILLS PRACTICED:	NOTES ON THE DRIVE:

TOTAL DRIVING TIME

Today's drive total		Accumulated Time	

SIGNATURE OF ADULT:

_____

Daily Driving Report

DATE: _____

LOCATION OF DRIVE: _____

SKILLS PRACTICED:	NOTES ON THE DRIVE:

TOTAL DRIVING TIME

Today's drive total		Accumulated Time	

SIGNATURE OF ADULT:

_____

Daily Driving Report

DATE: _____

LOCATION OF DRIVE: _____

SKILLS PRACTICED:	NOTES ON THE DRIVE:

TOTAL DRIVING TIME

Today's drive total		Accumulated Time	

SIGNATURE OF ADULT:

_____

Daily Driving Report

DATE:

LOCATION OF DRIVE:

SKILLS
PRACTICED:

NOTES ON THE
DRIVE:

TOTAL DRIVING TIME

Today's
drive
total

Accumulated
Time

SIGNATURE OF ADULT:

Daily Driving Report

DATE: _____

LOCATION OF DRIVE: _____

SKILLS PRACTICED:	NOTES ON THE DRIVE:

TOTAL DRIVING TIME

Today's drive total		Accumulated Time	

SIGNATURE OF ADULT:

_____

Daily Driving Report

DATE: _____

LOCATION OF DRIVE: _____

SKILLS PRACTICED:	NOTES ON THE DRIVE:

TOTAL DRIVING TIME

Today's drive total		Accumulated Time	

SIGNATURE OF ADULT:

_____

Daily Driving Report

DATE: _____

LOCATION OF DRIVE: _____

SKILLS PRACTICED:	NOTES ON THE DRIVE:

TOTAL DRIVING TIME

Today's drive total		Accumulated Time	

SIGNATURE OF ADULT:

_____

Daily Driving Report

DATE: _____

LOCATION OF DRIVE: _____

SKILLS PRACTICED:	NOTES ON THE DRIVE:

TOTAL DRIVING TIME

Today's drive total		Accumulated Time	

SIGNATURE OF ADULT:

_____

Daily Driving Report

DATE: _____

LOCATION OF DRIVE: _____

SKILLS PRACTICED:	NOTES ON THE DRIVE:

TOTAL DRIVING TIME

Today's drive total		Accumulated Time	

SIGNATURE OF ADULT:

_____

Daily Driving Report

DATE: _____

LOCATION OF DRIVE: _____

SKILLS PRACTICED:	NOTES ON THE DRIVE:

TOTAL DRIVING TIME

Today's drive total		Accumulated Time	

SIGNATURE OF ADULT:

_____

Daily Driving Report

DATE: _____

LOCATION OF DRIVE: _____

SKILLS PRACTICED:	NOTES ON THE DRIVE:

TOTAL DRIVING TIME

Today's drive total		Accumulated Time	

SIGNATURE OF ADULT:

_____

Daily Driving Report

DATE:

LOCATION OF DRIVE:

SKILLS
PRACTICED:

NOTES ON THE
DRIVE:

TOTAL DRIVING TIME

Today's
drive
total

Accumulated
Time

SIGNATURE OF ADULT:

Daily Driving Report

DATE: _____

LOCATION OF DRIVE: _____

SKILLS
PRACTICED:

NOTES ON THE
DRIVE:

TOTAL DRIVING TIME

Today's
drive
total

Accumulated
Time

SIGNATURE OF ADULT:

_____

Daily Driving Report

DATE: _____

LOCATION OF DRIVE: _____

SKILLS PRACTICED:	NOTES ON THE DRIVE:

TOTAL DRIVING TIME

Today's drive total		Accumulated Time	

SIGNATURE OF ADULT:

_____

Daily Driving Report

DATE: _____

LOCATION OF DRIVE: _____

SKILLS PRACTICED:	NOTES ON THE DRIVE:

TOTAL DRIVING TIME

Today's drive total		Accumulated Time	

SIGNATURE OF ADULT:

_____

Daily Driving Report

DATE:

LOCATION OF DRIVE:

SKILLS
PRACTICED:

NOTES ON THE
DRIVE:

TOTAL DRIVING TIME

Today's
drive
total

Accumulated
Time

SIGNATURE OF ADULT:

Daily Driving Report

DATE: _____

LOCATION OF DRIVE: _____

SKILLS PRACTICED:	NOTES ON THE DRIVE:

TOTAL DRIVING TIME

Today's drive total		Accumulated Time	

SIGNATURE OF ADULT:

_____

Daily Driving Report

DATE:

LOCATION OF DRIVE:

SKILLS PRACTICED:

NOTES ON THE DRIVE:

TOTAL DRIVING TIME

Today's drive total

Accumulated Time

SIGNATURE OF ADULT:

Daily Driving Report

DATE: _____

LOCATION OF DRIVE: _____

SKILLS PRACTICED:	NOTES ON THE DRIVE:

TOTAL DRIVING TIME

Today's drive total		Accumulated Time	

SIGNATURE OF ADULT:

_____

Daily Driving Report

DATE:

LOCATION OF DRIVE:

SKILLS PRACTICED:

NOTES ON THE DRIVE:

TOTAL DRIVING TIME

Today's drive total		Accumulated Time	

SIGNATURE OF ADULT:

Daily Driving Report

DATE: _____

LOCATION OF DRIVE: _____

SKILLS PRACTICED:	NOTES ON THE DRIVE:

TOTAL DRIVING TIME

Today's drive total		Accumulated Time	

SIGNATURE OF ADULT:

_____

Daily Driving Report

DATE: _____

LOCATION OF DRIVE: _____

SKILLS PRACTICED:	NOTES ON THE DRIVE:

TOTAL DRIVING TIME

Today's drive total		Accumulated Time	

SIGNATURE OF ADULT:

_____

Daily Driving Report

DATE: _____

LOCATION OF DRIVE: _____

SKILLS PRACTICED:	NOTES ON THE DRIVE:

TOTAL DRIVING TIME

Today's drive total		Accumulated Time	

SIGNATURE OF ADULT:

_____

Daily Driving Report

DATE: _____

LOCATION OF DRIVE: _____

SKILLS PRACTICED:	NOTES ON THE DRIVE:

TOTAL DRIVING TIME

Today's drive total		Accumulated Time	

SIGNATURE OF ADULT:

_____

Daily Driving Report

DATE: _____

LOCATION OF DRIVE: _____

SKILLS PRACTICED:	NOTES ON THE DRIVE:

TOTAL DRIVING TIME

Today's drive total		Accumulated Time	

SIGNATURE OF ADULT:

_____

Daily Driving Report

DATE: _____

LOCATION OF DRIVE: _____

SKILLS PRACTICED:	NOTES ON THE DRIVE:

TOTAL DRIVING TIME

Today's drive total		Accumulated Time	

SIGNATURE OF ADULT:

_____

Daily Driving Report

DATE: _____

LOCATION OF DRIVE: _____

SKILLS PRACTICED:	NOTES ON THE DRIVE:

TOTAL DRIVING TIME

Today's drive total		Accumulated Time	

SIGNATURE OF ADULT:

_____

Daily Driving Report

DATE:

LOCATION OF DRIVE:

SKILLS PRACTICED:	NOTES ON THE DRIVE:

TOTAL DRIVING TIME

Today's drive total		Accumulated Time	

SIGNATURE OF ADULT:

Daily Driving Report

DATE:

LOCATION OF DRIVE:

SKILLS
PRACTICED:

NOTES ON THE
DRIVE:

TOTAL DRIVING TIME

Today's
drive
total

Accumulated
Time

SIGNATURE OF ADULT:

Made in the USA
Middletown, DE
10 October 2023

40527272R00061